Hunting with My Dad

By Tony Vincent

Library For All Ltd.

LIBRARY FOR ALL

DIGITAL EDUCATION · FOR THE WORLD

Library For All is an Australian not for profit organisation with a mission to make knowledge accessible to all via an innovative digital library solution. Visit us at libraryforall.org

Hunting with My Dad

First published 2023

Published by Library For All Ltd
Email: info@libraryforall.org
URL: libraryforall.org

Our Yarning logo design by Jason Lee, Bidjipidji Art

Original illustrations by Fariza Dzatalin Nurtsani

Hunting with My Dad
Vincent, Tony
ISBN: 978-1-923143-38-8
SKU04323

Hunting with My Dad

We respect and honour Aboriginal and Torres Strait Islander Elders past, present and future. We acknowledge the stories, traditions and living cultures of Aboriginal and Torres Strait Islander peoples on this land and commit to building a brighter future together.

Sometimes after school, I go hunting with my dad.

It's so exciting to go hunting!

I always have a few jobs to do before Dad gets home.

If I get all the gear ready, we can go as soon as he arrives.

Yah!

Dad is home from work and all the gear is ready.

We pack the car and head off to the billabong.

When we get there, Dad parks the car.

After getting our gear, we go to wait for the geese to start flying over.

It is not long before a flock flies over us.

Dad takes two shots.

BANG! BANG!

One bird falls and I run over to collect it.

In the end, we get six geese and that is all we need.

Dad always says that we should never take more than we need.

Dad makes a fire so we can boil water. It helps us clean and pluck the birds, and it makes a strong damp smell.

Dad and I get to work.

After we finish cleaning, we cook one goose over some hot coals.

Yummy, yummy!

We put out the fire and head for home.

Everyone gets fresh goose for dinner tonight.

I love going hunting with my dad.

You can use these questions to talk about this book with your family, friends and teachers.

What did you learn from this book?

Describe this book in one word. Funny? Scary? Colourful? Interesting?

How did this book make you feel when you finished reading it?

What was your favourite part of this book?

download our reader app
getlibraryforall.org

About the author

Tony was born and lives in Darwin. He loved going out hunting with his dad when he was little, and takes his own family out to spend time in the bush, too.

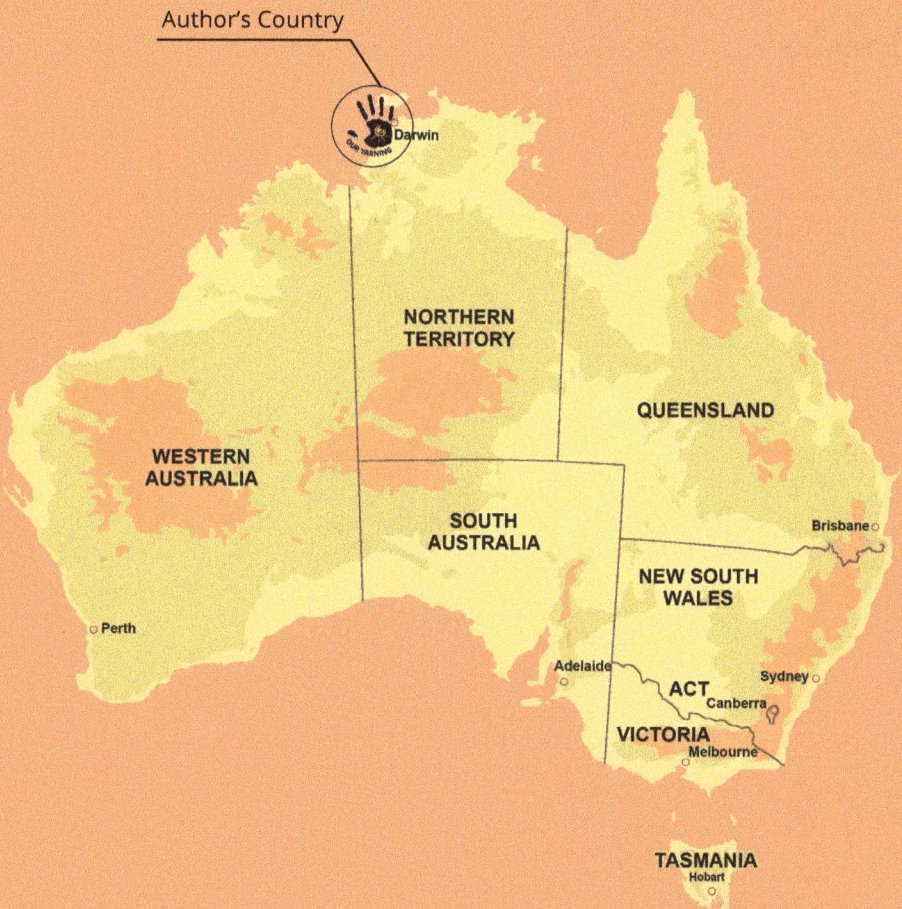

Author's Country

Darwin

NORTHERN
TERRITORY

QUEENSLAND

WESTERN
AUSTRALIA

SOUTH
AUSTRALIA

Brisbane

NEW SOUTH
WALES

Perth

Adelaide

Sydney

ACT
Canberra

VICTORIA
Melbourne

TASMANIA
Hobart

Our Yarning

Want to discover more books from this collection? Our Yarning is a collection of books written by Aboriginal and Torres Strait Islander peoples across Australia.

We know that children learn better, and enjoy reading more, when they see themselves in the stories, characters and illustrations of the books they read.

To download the app, visit the Google Play Store on any Android device and search 'Our Yarning'.

libraryforall.org